SCIENCE -5
DAV & NCERT

KRIVAANSH EDUTECH

XpressPublishing
An Imprint of Notion Press

No.8, 3rd Cross Street, CIT Colony,
Mylapore, Chennai, Tamil Nadu-600004

Copyright © Krivaansh Edutech
All Rights Reserved.

ISBN 978-1-64919-834-1

This book has been published with all efforts taken to make the material error-free after the consent of the author. However, the author and the publisher do not assume and hereby disclaim any liability to any party for any loss, damage, or disruption caused by errors or omissions, whether such errors or omissions result from negligence, accident, or any other cause.

While every effort has been made to avoid any mistake or omission, this publication is being sold on the condition and understanding that neither the author nor the publishers or printers would be liable in any manner to any person by reason of any mistake or omission in this publication or for any action taken or omitted to be taken or advice rendered or accepted on the basis of this work. For any defect in printing or binding the publishers will be liable only to replace the defective copy by another copy of this work then available.

This book is dedicated to my parents who always encourage me to do the best in life. My parents are Pillars of my life...

Thanks a ton

Mummy (Smt. Shanti Devi)

&

Papa (Shri Harish Chander Sharma)

Contents

Acknowledgements	*vii*
1. My Body	1
2. Plants	4
3. Forest	8
4. Animals Our Friends	12
5. Food And Health	16
6. Food Preservation	20
7. Importance Of Water	24
8. Properties Of Water	28
9. Fuels	30
10. Air	35
11. Solar System	39
12. Observing The Sky	43
13. Practice Test	46

Acknowledgements

About KRIVAANSH EDUTECH

KRIVAANSH EDUTECH provides all solved questions as per NCERT & DAV exercise and others important question for class V, VI, VII and VIII. We are very much sure it helps students to learn about the world in a better way. Because of this subject, students can get actual facts behind each and every incident in their daily life like the formation of a rainbow, gravitation, cooking, etc.

CHAPTER ONE

My Body

Ques 1:- Fill in the blanks:-

1. Wind pipe connects nose to the **Lungs** in mammals
2. Of the jaws. Only the **Lower jaw** moves.
3. The backbone protects the **Spinal cord**.
4. Fish can feel waves with the help of their **lateral line**
5. A snake uses its **tongue** to touch and smell objects.
6. Eye is connected to the brain by the **Optic Nerve**.
7. The joint in the shoulder is an example of a **ball and Socket Joint**.
8. The rib cage protects **our lungs & heart**.
9. Light enters the eye through **the pupil.**
10. The part of ear which helps in maintaining balance of our body **is inner ear**.
11. The rib cage have **12** pair of ribs.
12. Human backbone is made up of **33 vertebrae**.
13. Human skull is made up of **8 flat bones**.
14. Total number of bones in human body **is 206.**
15. Human have **230** joints in their body.
16. The smallest bone is **stirrup** and largest bone **is femur**.
17. **Bone marrow** is known as the factory for making blood cells.
18. **Arthritis** is a disease that causes joints pain, swelling and swiftness.
19. **Skin** is the largest sense organ of our body.

20. Human tongue has 9000 taste buds.

Ques 2:- Match the follows:-

1. Elbow   à   Hinge Joint
2. Wrist   à   Gliding Joint
3. Hip   à   Ball & Socket Joint
4. Femur   à   Longest Bone
5. Skull   à   Eight flat Bones

Q3. What is breathing?
Ans. The process of taking oxygen and give out carbon dioxide is called breathing.

Q4. How are fore limbs connected to the spine?
Ans. The fore limbs are connected to the spine by the shoulder girdles and collar bones.

Q5. State the importance of rib cage in our body?
Ans. The rib cage protects the inner delicate organs like heart, lungs.

Q6. Name the main parts of skeleton system?
Ans. The main parts of skeleton system are -:-

1. Skull   2. Rib cage   3. The back bone   4. The Limbs.

Q7. State the role of inner ear in the process of hearing?
Ans. The inner ear help us to hear & maintain balance in our body..

Q8. How a snake does detect the presence of an enemy or a prey?
Ans. The snake feels different kinds of vibrations on the earth through its skin. This helps it to detect the presence of any enemy or a prey.

Q9. Why do we have joints?
Ans. Joints allows movements of bones in different ways.

Q10. Why is our backbone made up of many small vertebrae instead of having one straight bone?
Ans. These small vertebrae give flexibility to our back.

Q11. Why is bone marrow known as the factory for making blood cells?
Ans. Blood cells are manufactured inside the bone marrow. Therefore, bone marrow is known as factory for making blood cells.

Q12. How does a ball and socket joint work?
Ans. In ball and socket joint, one bone which has ball like end, fits into the hollow socket of another bone. Eg. Hip and shoulder.

Q13. Do you breathe even when you are sleeping? Give reasons for your answer?
Ans. Yes, we breathe even when we are sleeping, because if the process of breathing stops for more than two minutes, the living being can die.

Q14. What is ultrasonics?
Ans. These are sounds that humans cannot hear.

CHAPTER TWO

Plants

Fill in the blanks:-

1. **Leaves** are known as food factories of the plants.
2. Plants, **Like Dahlia and Sweet Potato** reproduce through roots.
3. **Carbon Dioxide and Water** are raw materials needed for photosynthesis.
4. **Micropyle** is a small hole present in the seed.
5. Movement of seeds from one place to another is called **seed dispersal**
6. The small baby plant coming out of a seed is known as the **Seedling**.
7. The process, by which a plant make its own food is known as **Photosynthesis**.
8. Photo **means Light** and Synthesis means **" Putting Together"**.
9. **Stomata** are the tiny pores present on the leaf surface.
10. Indian Scientist **Prof. J. C. Bose** proved that plants have life.
11. Prof J. C. Bose invented an instrument called **crescograph**, used to measure **growth** of plant.
12. **Seed coat** is the thick outer covering of the seed which protect baby plant.

Match the following:-

1. Type of reproduction without seeds   -->   Banana
2. Green pigment present in leaves   -->   chlorophyll

3. A fruit that does not bear seeds --> Vegetative reproduction
4. Reproduction through leaves --> Bryophyllum
5. Dispersal of seeds through cracking --> Pea and Ladyfinger.

Answer the following Questions?

Q1. Name the pigment present in green leaves of a plant?
Ans. Chlorophyll is present in the green leaves of the plant.

Q2. Why do some plants feed on insects?
Ans. Some plants feeds on insect:-

1. These plants grow in poor soil which lacs nitrogen salts.
2. They get extra nourishment form insects. Like:- Venus flytrap and Pitcher plant.

Q3. Name the two methods of reproduction in plants?
Ans. 1. Reproduction through seed. (eg. Wheat, rice, maize)
    2. Reproduction through different parts of plants stem, root, leaf.

Q4. State the condition required for the proper germination of a seed?
Ans. 1. Air,   2. Water,   3. Warmth Temperature

Q5. Name the two plants that reproduce through stem cutting?
Ans. Banana, Potato, and Ginger.

Q6. Why do all seed not germinate to form new plants?
Ans. Seed which get favourable conditions like appropriate air, water, soil and proper temperature required to grow to form a new plant.

Q7. State the importance of vegetative reproduction in plants?
Ans. 1. It is an easier and faster method of increasing number of the same plants.

1. It also helps to grow plants like, banana , Like bear no seed.

Q8. State the function of the following:-
Ans 1.<u>Seed Coat</u>: <u>Seed coat</u>is the thick outer covering of the seed which protect baby plant.

2. <u>Cotyledons</u>: - The seed leaves inside the seed coat is cotyledons. It store food for baby plant to grow.
3. <u>Micropyle:</u>- <u>Micropyle</u>is a small hole present in the seed. It allows water to enter inside.

Q9.Write the ways of dispersal of seeds in the following plants:-

1. <u>Madar</u> :- Dispersal by wind.
2. <u>Lotus</u>:- Dispersal by water.
3. <u>Castor</u>:- Dispersal by human and animals.
4. <u>Beans</u>:- Dispersal through cracking or bursting.
5. <u>Mango</u>:- Dispersal by human and animals.
6. <u>Water Lilly</u>:- Dispersal by water.
7. <u>Rose Plant</u>:- Using the stem Cutting of growing up Plant.

Q10. Seeds do not germinate when they are kept in an ice box or fridge?
Ans. Seeds do not germinate when they are kept in an ice box because they need favourable temperature warmth for germination.

Q11. **Give one example of each:-**
Insectivorous Plant -->Venus flytrap, pitcher plant
Plant having one cotyledon --> Wheat, rice, maize
Plant having two cotyledon--> Pea, gram , beans
Reproduction through underground stem -->Ginger, potato
Reproduction by stem cutting --> Rose, grape, sugarcane
Reproduction by leaf --> Bryophyllum,
Reproduction by root--> Sweet potato, dahlia,

Q12. Name the natural agents that enable the seed to move from one place to another?
Ans. Human, animal, birds, wind, water, insects, rodents etc.

Q13. What is reproduction?
Ans. The process by which a living thing produces more of its own kind is called reproduction.

CHAPTER THREE

Forest

Fill in the blanks:-

A. **Forest** Serve as home to many types of animals.
B. Forest absorbs large amounts **of Carbon Dioxide**gas.
C. **Deforestation**decrease rainfall in the surrounding areas.
D. **Bharatpur Bird Sanctuary**is the largest Bird Sanctuary in Asia.
E. For early man, forest were a source of **food and shelter.**
F. The leaf, used to make disposable plates is the **areca nut leaf**.
G. Deforestation result in **Soil erosion**.
H. Bee wax is used to make **medicines**.
A. Tendu leaf is also known as **Green Gold of Odisha**.
J. A **forest**is an area where the earth is covered mainly by large number of trees.
K. **A Sanctuary**is reserved area in which birds and animal are protected from hunting.
L. The Forest Conservation Act was enacted by **the Indian Parliament in 1980.**
M. **Gir National Park**is the only place for Asiatic Lions is protected.
N. **Van Mahotsava**is a program launched by Indian Govt. to increase the number of trees.
O. Chipko Andolan literally means "**Hug the Trees**".

Match the following.

1. Resins   --> Paint
2. Forests   --> Soil conservators
3. Deforestation --> Cutting down of trees
4. Aswagandha --> Medicinal plant
5. Gums   --> Adhesives

Q1. Name any four products that are obtained from forests?
Ans. Bamboo, Sandal Wood, Gums, Rubber, Lac etc.
Q2. Why do some men cut trees?
Ans. Men cut forest because of the following reasons:-

1. Need more land to make houses, industries, and for agriculture.
2. Needs wood for construction.

Q3. What is the Gir National Park famous for?
Ans. Gir national Park is famous for the Asiatic Lions.
Q4. Name two migratory Birds that visit Bharatpur Bird Sanctuary?
Ans. 1. Siberian Cranes, Barons, Ibis, Painted Storks.
Q5. What is the average temperature and annual rainfall needed for a forest?
Ans. Forest develops at place where the average temperature is greater than 10° C and where there is an annual rainfall of at least 200mm.
Q6. List four harmful effects of deforestation.
Ans. 1. Decrease in rainfall
 2 Increase in the amount of carbon dioxide in the atmosphere that can increase global warming.
 3 Decrease in the levels of ground water in the nearby areas.
 4 Increase in soil erosion that can cause more frequent floods.
Q7. How do forest prevent soil erosion?
Ans. Forest prevent soil erosion as trees bind soil particles with their strong roots. This prevent soil from being washed or blown away.
Q8. State the importance of forest to human beings?

Ans. 1. Trees purify the air by absorbing carbon dioxide and releasing oxygen.

2 Forest help to bring good rainfall.

3 Forest prevent soil erosion.

4 Trees also help in checking the global warming by absorbing carbon dioxide which is main greenhouse gas.

Q9. Why the forests known as the "Lungs of earth"?

Ans. Forest are earth's air purifiers. They are often referred to as the earth's lungs. Just as our lungs abrob carbon dioxide from the blood and infuse it with oxygen, green plants absorb carbon dioxide during photosynthesis and in return , release oxygen into the atmosphere.

Q10. How can we contribute toward protection of forest?

Ans. 1 By minimizing the use of wood and wood protects.

2 By not using products that promote destruction of forests.

3 By celebrating the growing of plants as a festival and involving more and more people in this activity..

Q11. What is deforestation?

Ans:- Larges scale cutting of trees is called deforestation.

Fill ups:-

1. Deforestation result in **Soil erosion, low rainfall and flood**.
2. Only **20%** of the world's ancient forests are left.
3. A light weight narrow boat is **Canoe**
4. If forests disappear, the amount of carbon dioxide in air **will increase**.
5. Migratory Birds:- Siberian Cranes, Barons
6. National Parks :- Kaziranga, Gir
7. Birds Sanctuary :- Bharatpur, Chilka
8. Medicinal Plantts:- Amla, Ashwagandha

KRIVAANSH EDUTECH

CHAPTER FOUR

Animals Our Friends

Fill in the blanks:-

1. We keep **dogs** and cats as pet.
2. **Dogs** assist police in search operations.
3. **Kasturi** is an ingredients of musk deer.
4. Task of elephant have been used for making **jewellery.**
5. Extinction of frogs will increase the **Insects** populations.
6. Food chains are found in all **Habitats**.
7. **PETA** stands for people for Ethical Treatment of Animals.
8. Food chain is a process of **"who eats whom"**.
9. **Kenya's Masai mara**, is world's famous wildlife sanctuaries.
10. Elephants are hunted for their **tusk.**
11. A delicacy made from the unfertiliseed eggs of a variety of fish is the **caviar**.
12. **Quagga** animal is extinct.
13. Humans are destroying habitat of animals by **cutting down the trees**.

Match the column:-
Silk --> Silkworm
Elephants -->Tusk, jwelllery
Wool --> Sheep
North & south American bears--> Gall bladderà medicines

Leather --> Skin of goat, sheep, buffalo
Rhinoceroses--> Hornsàmedicine
pearls--> Oysters
Musk deer--> Kasturi—perfumes
transport --> Horse, camel, elephant, Ox
Mountain goats --> Hair yield—Pashmina
Sea food --> Crab
Tiger --> Bones & Skin

Keywords:-
Draught animals --> An animal used for pulling heavy loads.
Endangered --> In danger of becoming extinct.
Extinct --> When no members of a species exists any longer.
Habitat --> A place where certain kind of plant grow & animals live.
Oysters --> A type of shell fish ahs a rough shell with two parts, it is eaten both cooked & raw.
Pollute --> Make dirty.
Species --> A group of very similar plants or animals.
Tusk --> Extra long tooth that grow outside the moth of elephant.
Veterinarian --> Doctor that looks after, heals & treats animals.

Q1. Name five wild animals?
Ans.. Monitor lizard, Elephant, Wild boar, Tiger, Giraffe

Q2. Give the meaning of term "food chain"?
Ans. Food chain is the process of "who eats whom".

Q3. How are human beings destroying the natural surroundings of wild animals?
Ans. Human beings are destroying the natural surroundings of wild animals by cutting down the forest & by polluting rivers.

Q4. Name the animals that can become man eaters?
Ans. Tiger & Leopard can become the man eaters.

Q5. Which act has been passed by the Indian Government to protect wildlife?/

Ans. Government of India enacted the wildlife protection Act 1972, with the objective of effective controlling poaching & illegal trade in wildlife.

Q6. Name any two products obtained from animals?
Ans. Milk & eggs.

Q7. How compost is useful for plants?
Ans. Compost is useful for plants for their growth & make soil fertile.

Q8. Why some animals become extinct?
Ans. Human beings are destroying the natural surroundings of animals due to this many animals are not able to live their changed surroundings are become extinct.

Q9. What is food web?
Ans. Interconnected food chains form a web.

Q10. What do you know about PETA?
Ans. People for the Ethical Treatment of Animals are an animal right organization. It is the largest animal rights group in the world. The main aim of organization is to stop violence against animals.

Q11. Difference between the endangered and extinct?
Ans.

Extinct Animals -->Animals species which are no longer living are called extinct animals . Eg. Quagga, passenger pigeon, golden tood etc.

Endangered Animals --> Animals species which are in danger of becoming extinct are called endangered animals. Eg. African Elephants, bald eagle etc.

Q 12. What is wildlife trade? Why it is harmful?
Ans. The animals which are being killed because their body parts are used by humans. This is known as wildlife trade. If this type of illegal trade continues, many species may disappear from the earth.

Q13. Suggest any four ways to prevent cruelty to animals?

Ans. 1. Do not throw polythene bags in the garbage. Stray cattle can swallow them & they may be die.
2. Do not put birds in cage and fist in aquarium.
3. When visiting a forest, park or garden one should not remove eggs of birds from their nest.
4. If you have pets, give them the love & good care that they deserve if the pet animal appears to be sick, take it to the veterinarian.

CHAPTER FIVE

Food and Health

Fill in the blanks:-

1. A **disease** is any defect or abnormality found in the body.
2. Children, in the age group of **6 months to 3 year**, often suffer from protein-carbohydrate deficiency disease.
3. Minerals are present in **small** amount in our body.
4. The disease, that cause enlargement of glands in the neck, is known as **Goitre.**
5. The disease that get spred through insects, air, water, and soil is known as **communicable diseases**.
6. Haemoglobin content become less when a person is suffering from **anaemia.**
7. A person having swollen & bleeding gums, might be suffering from **Scurvy.**
8. Germs of common cold spread through **air.**
9. Legs become bow shaped due to deficiency of **Vitamin D.**

10 Deficiency of proteins & carbohydrate in the diet of small child can lead to **improper growth of body.**

11 **Haemoglobin** is the pigment found in the blood which transport oxygen & provide red color blood.

12 **Vitamin B1**, was the first vitamin to be discovered.

13 **Nutrients** are the substance present in the food that is required for proper **growth & development** of the body.

14 Health is a state of complete **physical & mental** well being.

15 **Malnutrition** is a term used for a condition caused by improper or inadequate nourishment.

16 **Symptoms** are sign that indicate a disease.

17 **Vaccination** must be done to prevent disease like measles, polio etc.

18 **Balanced diet** contains all type of nutrients.

Match the column:-

1. Protein --> body building food.
2. Carbohydrate --> energy giving food.
3. Fats --> provide energy & warmth.
4. Vitamin & minerals --> proper functioning of body.
5. Iron --> Anaemia
6. Iodine --> Goitre
7. Vitamin A --> Night blindness
8. Vitamin B --> Beri- Beri
9. Vitamin C --> Scurvy
10. Vitamin D --> Rickets
11. Disease spread by insects --> malaria & dengue
12. Disease spread by water, air, soil --> coughing, sneezing, measles, chickenpox.

Q/A

Q1. Name two main categories of diseases?
Ans. Communicable & Non-Communicable

Q2. Name two symptoms of disease beri-beri?
Ans. 1. Extra weakness.   2. Paralysis of body part.

Q3. Write any two diseases that are spread through bite of mosquitos?
Ans. Dengue, malaria

Q4. A girl find it difficult to see in dim light and has dry scaly skin. Name the disease she might be suffering from?
Ans. Night blindness.

Q5. Why should we not allow water to stagnate around our houses?
Ans. We should not allow water to stagnate around our houses because stagnate water is breeding place of mosquitoes.

Q6. How does calcium-phosphorus deficiency affect our body?
Ans. Calcium- phosphorus deficiency defect our body as :-

1. Weak teeth lose their shine and whiteness.
2. Weak, soft and fragile bones.

Q7. Suggest some measure that can help us to prevent the occurrence of deficiency disease?
Ans. The deficiency disease can be prevented by adopting the following measure:-

1. One should take a balance diet containing all type of nutrients.
2. One must follow good food practice and habits.
3. Children must be given adequate amount of milk and additional food items like juices, rice etc.

Q8. How can we prevent the spread of germs from a sick person to a healthy person?
Ans. Communicable disease can be prevented by observing the following ways:-

1. All the articles and clothes of infected person should be disinfected.

2. One must always cover the nose or mouth while sneezing or coughing.
3. The surroundings must be kept clean and hygienic.

Q9. Isha was suffering from chickenpox. Her teacher advised her not to come to school till she has recovered completely. Why?

Ans. Chicken pox is communicable disease it spread through air so Isha's teacher advised her not to come to school till she has recovered completely.

Q10. Why deficiency diseases are called non-communicable diseases?

Ans. Deficiency diseases are called non communicable diseases because this disease not transmitted from one person to another person.

CHAPTER SIX

Food Preservation

Question / Answer

Q1. State two factors that contribute to the fast growth of micro-organism?

Ans. Factors that contribute to the fast growth of micro-organism are:-

1. Moisture
2. Warmth Temperature.

Q2. What is likely to happen to the curd if it is not stored in the refrigerator?

Ans. Curd becomes sour if it is not stored in the refrigerator.

Q3. What do you understand by food preservation?

Ans. Food preservation is the process of treating and handling of food to stop, or slow down, the spoilage caused by Micro-organism.

Q4. How can we protect our food from insects, worms & rats?

Ans. To protect our food from insects, worms, and rats. We should stored the food items in clean & dry cupboard and containers.

Q5. Why does food stay fresh for a longer time when stored in a refrigerator?

Ans. Micro-organism and enzymes get deactivated at low temperature. So, food stay fresh fro longer time when stored in a refrigerator.

Long Q/A.

Q1. Give any three reasons for spoilage of food?
Ans. Three main reasons of spoilage of food are:-

1. Micro-organism
2. Enzymes
3. Insects, worms & rats.

Q2. How is food preservation useful for us?
Ans. Food preservation is useful for us in following ways:-

1. It helps to maintain nutritive value of food.
2. It increases the shelf life of food, thus increasing its supply. Many perishable foods can be preserved for a long time.
3. It makes seasonal foods available throughout the year.
4. It decreases wastage of food by preventing decay or spoilage of food.

Q3. Why it is important to check the manufacturing and the expiry date of packaged food items before consuming them?
Ans. It is important to do so because the food products that are packed remains fit for consuming, for a limited period.

Q4. Explain the following methods of food preservation:-
Ans. 1.**Dehydration**:- In this process, water content of the food stuff is removed. Since most micro-organism needs water to grow, they cannot multiply, or grow on dried foods.

2. **Caning & bottling**: - Canning involves cooking food, sealing it in sterile cans or jars, and bottling the containers to kill or weaken any remained bacteria through a form of sterilization.
3. **Pasteurization**:- It is the process in which the food product is subjected to pressurised heating, for a short time, followed by immediate cooling. The temperature used during pasteurization is below 212°F. Milk is pasteurized to kill micro-organism.

Q5. Rakesh bought two raw papayas. He kept one papaya in the refrigerator and other papaya on the kitchen shelf. Which will ripen first and why?

Ans. 1. The papaya which is kept on the kitchen shelf ripen faster because at room temperature enzymes become active.

2. The papaya which is kept in the refrigerator will take longer time to ripen because in low temperature enzymes get deactivated.

Keywords:-

Dehydration:- The process of removing water from a substance.

Enzymes:- Chemicals present in the fruits and vegetables which speed up the changes in them.

Food Preservation:- The process of treating, or handling, food to stop, or sllow down, its spoilage or decay.

Micro-Organism:- Organism, like bacteria and fungi, which are too small to be seen by unaided eye

Pasteurisation:- The process of heating food followed by immediate cooling, to limit the growth of micro- organism.

Fill in the blanks:-

1. Micro organism like bacteria and **fungi**spoil the food.
2. Insects make their home in **moist and dark**places.

3. Enzymes can be harmful because they can cause **spoilage** of fruits and vegetable.
4. Snacks, like biscuits and chips, should be stored in **airtight** jars.
5. The growth of micro-organism slows down at **low** temperature.
6. A natural insects repellant, found in our kitchen is **turmeric powder**.
7. Dry foods, like cereals and nuts are preserved **by vacuum packing**.
8. Fruits and vegetables get ripened due to the action of **enzymes**.
9. The changes of spoilage of food can be reduced by keeping the food at **low** temperature.
10. We should always drink fresh & **pasteurised** milk.
11. Pasteurisation **inactive** some enzymes & **increase** the shelf life of milk.
12. Preservation help to maintain **nutritive** value of food.

Match the following:-

1. Micro-organism --> Bacteria & Fungi
2. Enzymes --> Chemicals present in fruits.
3. Pasteurisation --> Louis Pasteur
4. Rancid Food --> change in taste and smell in presence of oxygen.
5. Food preservation --> way to handling food & stop decay & spoilage.
6. Acetic acid --> in form of vinegar.
7. Sugar & Salt --> preparing & preserving pickle & jam.
8. Dehyderation --> process of removing water from food stuff.

CHAPTER SEVEN

Importance of water

Keywords

1. **Amphibious animal**   -->animals which can live both in water or on land.
2. **Aquatic animal**   --> animals which live in water.
3. **Aquatic plants**   --> plants which grow in water.
4. **Ground water**   --> water which is trapped between underground rocks.
5. **Stepwell**   --> a well which has steps on its wall..

Ques/Ans.

Q1. Name any two water bodies that exist on the surface of the earth?
Ans. River, Lakes

Q2. What are animals living in water known as? Write names of two such animals?
Ans. Animals living in water are known as aquatic animals. Eg. Fish, Whale, Octopus etc.

Q3. What are amphibious animals?
Ans. Animals that can live both in water or on land are called amphibious animals. Eg. Frog, Turtle, Crocodile.

Q4. Name four aquatic plants?
Ans. Lotus, Water Lily, Hydrilla, Duckweed, water Lettuce, etc.

Q5. How do plants absorb water from the soil?
Ans. 1. Plants absorb water from the soil with the help of their roots.

2. This absorbed water transport the nutrients to various parts of the plants.

Q6. State two common methods of drawing out ground water?
Ans. Well and Handpump.

Q7. Besides its domestic use, state three other uses of water?
Ans. Water is also used for:-

1. Irrigating the fields.
2. Generating electricity
3. For transportation

Q8. How does water help in excretion of waste material from animal bodies?
Ans. 1. All animals drink water, the nutrients present in food get dissolved
in water.

2. This helps their bodies to absorb the nutrients
3. The animal body also produces waste material.
4. Some of these waste get dissolved in water and are excreted in from of urine.

Q9. List any four ways in which water is important for plants?
Ans. Importance of water for plants:-

1. Plants require various nutrients. These nutrients get dissolved in water present in soil.

2. Water help in transportation of nutrients to various parts of the plant.
3. Plant needs water for preparing their own food by the process of photosynthesis.
4. Plants require water for germinating seeds.
5. Water is a habitat for many plants..

Q10. How can ground water be drowning out through tube wells?
Ans. Ground water is also drawn out using tube well. In a tube well, a long pipe is inserted deep into the ground where it dips below the ground water level. Water is then drawn up by using hand pump or electric pump.

Q11. What is a step well?
Ans. 1. A step well is a well having steps on its all sides.
   2. This enables people to go down to fetch water.

Q12. How is water supplied in cities?
Ans. 1. Now a days there are well planned water supply system in cities.
   2. In such a system the rivers water is usually purified by a series of processes that make it fit for drinking.
   3. This purifies water is then sent at homes and offices through a network of pump and pipes.

Q13. Why water is important for plants & Animals?
Ans. Water is essential for the existence and survival of plants & animals.

Q14. There is so much of water around but yet less available for living beings? Justify?
Ans. We have learnt that three-fourth of the surface of earth is covered with water. However, only a very small percentage is used

by living beings because:-

1. 97% water is in sea and ocean.
2. Sea water is salty so it is not used by living beings.

Fill in the blanks:-

1. Water help in **digestion** of food in animals
2. Animals living in water are called **aquatic animals.**
3. Animals which can live both in water or land are called **amphibious animals.**
4. Water trapped between underground rocks is called **ground water.**
5. **Lotus and water Lilly** are aquatic plants.
6. About 97% of water is present in **seas and ocean.**
7. Plants absorb water from the soil with the help of **roots.**
8. A **rehat** is used for drawing out ground water for irrigation.
9. An example of an amphibious animal is **frog.**
10. Ground water can be drawn out using water wheel also known as **rehat**.
11. Actually a stem, often eaten as a vegetable **kamal kakri.**
12. Method to draw out ground water, from a well **pulley.**

CHAPTER EIGHT

Properties of Water

Keywords

Condensation --> Change of vapour form of a substance into liquid form on cooling.

Evaporation --> Change of a liquid into its vapour form.

Solute --> The substance that gets dissolve in a medium to form a solution.

Solution --> Mixture formed when a substance dissolve completely in any medium.

Solvent --> The medium in which a substance is dissolved to form a solution.

Transpiration --> It a process similar to evaporation. It is the loss of water from parts of plants, especially leaves. Transpiration add to the amount of water vapour present in the air. Thus it also play cloud formation

Fill in the blanks:-

1 A substance which is dissolve completely in a liquid is said to be **soluble** in it.

2 The substance that dissolves in a medium to form a solution is known as **Solvent**

3 Mustard oil is **insoluble** in water.

4 Aquatic animals breathe the **oxygen** gas dissolves in water.

5 Change of a liquid into its vapour form is called **evaporation**.

6 Condensation is the process of change of **vapour** into water.

7 Wet clothes get dried due to **evaporation**.

8 Mixture of sugar, salt, & lemon juice in a water is **a solution**.
9 Transpiration is process similar to **evaporation**.
10 The state of water can be change with the **temperature**.
11 Physical states of water **are liquid, solid, Gas (vapour)**.
12 The given material may sink or float in water depends on its **nature & type**.

Give one example of each:-

1. A gas which dissolve in water --> oxygen
2. A gas which does not dissolve in water --> Nitrogen
3. A substance which is soluble in water --> salt & Sugar
4. A substance which is insoluble in water -->marbles, sand, coins
5. A material which float on water --> cork, thermocole, hair oil.
6. Liquid which dissolve in water --> Milk & Ink
7. Liquid which are insoluble in water --> mustard oil & carbon Tetrachloride

1Q. How are clouds formed?
Ans. **1.**Water from water bodies changes into vapour as it evaporates due to the heat of the sun.
2. These water vapours go very high, they get cooled and condensed to form tiny droplets of liquid water.
In this way clouds are formed.

2Q. How does rain water get impure?
Ans. Rain water when reaches the surface of the earth become impure because many harmful gases, dust, and smoke present in air mix with rain water & make it impure.

3.Q. What is the importance of water cycle?
Ans. The cycle process of evaporation of water from the earth surface followed by its condensation maintain water balance in nature.

CHAPTER NINE

Fuels

Keywords

Biomass --> The waste matter of animals and plants.

CNG--> Compressed natural gas

Coal -->A black rock that is a type of fossil fuel.

Fossil fuel -->Fuels which are formed from decomposition of living things over a period of millions of years.

Fuel--> A substance that produces energy on burning

Green fuel --> Fuel which can causes less environmental pollution

LPG --> Liquefied petroleum gas

Non-renewable source of energy --> A source of energy likely to be available only for a limited period of time.

Petroleum --> Fossil fuel used mainly for transportation

PNG --> Piped natural gas

Renewable source of energy --> Sustainable source of energy likely to be always available.

Fill in the blanks:-

- **Food**acts as the fuel for our body.
- Cowdung cake has been often used as a **domestic**fuel.
- Aeroplanes as highly refined **kerosene**based fuel.
- **CNG**is better green fuel.
- Petrol & **diesel**are fossil fuels used for transportation.
- Solar energy is **renewable**source of energy.

- **LPG** is used as domestic fuel.
- A good fuel is that does not produce **smoke & leave ash**.
- A fuel that is obtaining by refining **petroleum** is kerosene.
- Fuel made by decomposition of animals and plants matter is **fossil fuel**.
- Electricity generated by the energy of water is called **hydroelectricity.**
- **Coal** is combustible black sedimentary rock.
- **Crude oil (petroleum)** is formed by Dead Sea creatures.
- Natural gas is collected when **drilling** for oil.
- Electricity is now being produced by **wind, sun & water.**
- Fuels are available in **solid, liquid and gaseous** forms.
- It is used as filler for golf balls **Coal Ash.**
- A place where coal is burned to convert water into **steam powerhouse**.
- **A combustible** black sedimentary rock Coal
- A green fuel **CNG**
- Used as fuel in aero planes **Aviation Turbine Fuel (ATF).**

Q1. State the main function of the fuel?
Ans. Fuel produces energy on burning.

Q2. Give one example each of solid, liquid, and gaseous fuels?
Ans. Solid fuel- wood, coal. Liquid fuel – Petrol, Diesel Gaseous Fuel- LPG, CNG

Q3. Why is biogas regarded as a better fuel than cow dung cake?
Ans. Biogas is a better fuel than cow dung cake because it does not produce smokes on burning and do not leave any ash after burning.

Q4. Why is CNG called a better green fuel?
Ans. CNG is called a better green fuel because:-

1. CNG vehicles have lower maintenance cost and better efficiency.
2. It causes less air pollution is more eco friendly and cause less harm to the health of human and animals.

Q5. State two disadvantages of fossil fuels?
Ans. 1. Fossil fuels are available in limited quantity and are not likely to last
for a long time.

2. They are also a major cause of environment pollution.

Q6. Name three main fossil fuels?
Ans. Natural Gas, Coal, Petroleum.

Q7. How fossil fuels been formed?
Ans. 1 Fossil fuels are formed by decomposition of animal and plants
matter, buried deep
under the surface of earth, at the high temperature and pressure.
2 Fossil fuels take millions of years to form.

Q8. When is a source of energy said to be a renewable source of energy? Give two examples of such resources?
Ans. Sources of energy which are freely available & which can be readily replenshied are called renewable sources of energy. Eg. Solar energy & tidal energy.

Q9. when is a source of energy said to be a non renewable source of energy? Give tow examples of such energy?
Ans. Sources of energy which once used, cannot be readily replenshied are called non renewable source of energy.. Eg. Coal & petroleum.

Q10. How is coal used by powerhouse for generating electricity?

Ans. Powerhouse often burn coal to convert water into steam. This stem energy is used to operate turbines which in turn, help to generate the electricity.

Q11. Why should efforts need to made to reduce the use of fossil fuels?

Ans. We should make suitable efforts to conserve fuel as :-

1. We can use cycle or walk to a near by place instead of going on a car or motorbike.
2. It is also desirable to from car- pool and to use public transport like buses, metro trains for travelling within the city.

Q12. What is biomass? Do you think it is a good option as a renewable source of energy? Justify?

Ans. The waste matter of animals & plants are called biomass. Yes, it is a good renewable source of energy.

Q13. What are some efforts taken by the government to reduce pollution?

Ans. 1. Plant more trees.

2. Less use of vehicles.
3. Use of green fuels.
4. Regular check up of pollutions.

Q14. Write full forms of :-

1. LPG -> liquid petroleum gas
2. CNG -->compressed natural gas
3. PNG --> Piped natural gas

4. ATF --> Aviated Turbine Fuel.

CHAPTER TEN

Air

KEYWORDS

Acid Rain --> Mixture of acidic gases with rain.

Composition --> Components present in a given substance.

Global warming --> Addition / extra increase in the average temperature of earth.

Green house effect --> Phenomenon which helps the earth to maintain its surface temperature.

Photosynthesis --> The process of making food by plants.

Water vapor --> Gaseous form of water.

Humidity --> The amount of water present in the air determines the humidity of the air.

Fill in the blanks:-

1 The two main gases present in the air are **Nitrogen and oxygen**.

2 Animals need **oxygen** gas for breathing

3 Plants use **carbon Dioxide** gas to prepare their own food.

4 The process by which plants prepare their own food is **photosynthesis**.

5 **Ozone** gas, present in the atmosphere protect us from the harmful rays of sunlight.

6 Air, containing impurities is **polluted air**.

7 The gas which is present most in the air is **nitrogen.**

8 An air pollutant which exists in solid form is **smoke**.

9 The gas whose amount varies with weather changes is **water vapour**.

10 The gas that gets reduced through the process of photosynthesis is **carbon dioxide**.

11 when sulphar dioxide reacts with water and oxygen in the air, it results in the production **of acid rain**.

12 On an average the human being breathes **22000 times**& takes about **16 Kg** of air everyday.

13 **Oxygen** is required for burning.

14 Two basic form of pollutants are **gaseous and solid**.

Q1. Name the main component of the air?
Ans. Air is mainly made up of nitrogen (78%) & oxygen (21%). It also contains 1% of water vapour and small amount of other gases.

Q2. State two harmful effect of ultraviolet rays?
Ans. 1. Ultraviolet rays can cause skin & eye diseases in animals.
2. these rays can also affect the growth of plants.

Q3. Define air pollutants?
Ans. The impurities present the air is called air pollutant.

Q4. List any two gaseous & solid pollutants present in the air?
Ans. Gaseous :- carbon monoxide, sulphar, nitrogen oxide.
    Solid :- dust, germs, smoke.

Q5. List any four causes of air pollution?
Ans. 1. Smoke from forest fires.
    2. germs from cough & sneezing.
    3. smoke emitted from vehicles.
    4. dust raised from the ground during dust storms.

Q6. Why is air necessary for animals?
Ans. 1. All the animals, including humans being need oxygen to live.

2. They take oxygen from air through the process of breathing.

3. The oxygen, present in the air, is used to produce energy from the food that is eaten.

Q7. How is nitrogen important for plants?

Ans. 1. Nitrogen gas present in the air is essential for the growth of the palnts.

2. it also helps them to develop their fruit & seeds.

3. it increase the size & quality of their leaves.

Therefore, plants require large amount of nitrogen.

Q8. How is the balance of oxygen & carbon dioxide in air, maintained in nature?

Ans. 1. Animals & human being use oxygen present in the air & give out carbon dioxide gas.

2. Plants on other hand consume carbon dioxide during photosynthesis in day time.

3. Then they give out oxygen.'

In this way, a balance of carbon dioxide and oxygen is maintained in the air.

Q9. Why acid rain is harmful?

Ans. Acid rain damages crops & reduces the fertility of soil. It can also damage monuments made up of marbles.

Q10. Why should we feel worried about the global warming?

Ans. 1. Extra increase in the average temperature of the earth.

2. This can result in increase in the melting of polar ice caps which can cause wide spread damage & destruction.

Q11. Suggest some ways to reducing air pollution?

Ans. 1. We should plant more trees.

2. Lesser use of vehicles

3. Regular checkups of vehicles.

4. Use of cleaner Fuels like CNG, biogas, LPG
5. Dumping of garbage in the pit.
6. Constructing tall chimneys.

Q12. How does planting of trees help in making air cleaner?

Ans. Plants use up carbon dioxide gas present in the sir, for producing their food using photosynthesis. This helps to reduce the greenhouse effect & maintain the earth's temperature at a desirable level.

CHAPTER ELEVEN

Solar System

Fill in the blanks:-

1 The earth is sometimes known as **Blue** Planet.

2 The earth complete one rotation about its axis in **24** Hours.

3 The main member of our solar system are the sun and **eight** planets.

4 The sun is a huge source of **light & heat**.

5 Day and night occurs on earth due to **its rotation** about its own axis.

6 The number of planet, in our solar system **is 8**.

7 The planet, which reflects large amount of sunlight falling on it is **Venus**.

8 The planet Uranus is also known as **Jovian** Planet.

9 **Aryabhatta** is the First Indian satellite launched in 1975.

10 **Moon** is the natural satellite.

11 The earth completes one revolutions around the sun in nearly **365** days.

12 Neptune is known as the **Windy** planet.

13 The planet Saturn is known **as ringed** planet.

14 Moon reflects the light received from the **Sun.**

15 **Mercury, Venus and mars** are known as Terrestrial Planets.

16 An airless planet with contrasting cold and hot regions **Mercury**.

17 A **day** for a planet equals the time taken by it to complete one rotation on its axis.

18 A year for a planet equals the time taken to complete one revolution around the sun.

Match the following:-

1. Red planet --> Mars.
2. Largest planet --> Jupiter
3. Planet sustaining life --> earth
4. Natural satellite --> moon
5. The windy planet --> Neptune
6. The smallest planet --> Mercury
7. The ringed planet --> Saturn
8. Artificial satellite of India --> Rohini, apple, INSAT, EAUSAT, Chandrayan-1, Gst -4
9. Rotation --> earth's spinning about its own axis.
10. Revolution --> earth's orbital motion around the sun.

Question / Answer

Q1. Name the hottest planet in our solar system. Is it close to the sun?
Ans. The hottest planet of solar system is Venus. No, it is not close to the sun.

Q2. State the nature of the shape of orbit of planets?
Ans. The shape of orbit planet is elliptical.

Q3. Write the meaning of "Artificial Satellite"?
Ans. Artificial satellites are man-made objects, which can be made to revolve around the earth.

Q4. How is sun useful to us?
Ans. Sun is useful for us in many ways:-

1. The sun is a source of huge energy.
2. It gives out energy in the form of heat and light.
3. The sun is essential for growth & maintenance of all forms of life on the earth.
4. Plants, animals depend on the sun for their food.
5. Solar energy is used in solar cooker and solar geysers.

Q5. Name the terrestrial planets. Why are the so called?

Ans. Mercury, Venus, earth & Mars are mostly made of rocks and metals. So they are called terrestrial planets.

Q6. State the condition necessary for existence of life on a planet?

Ans. The conditions necessary for existence of life on a planet are:-

1. Presence of atmosphere.
2. Presence of liquid (water) on the surface.
3. Right size and right distance from the sun that enables it to receive just the correct amount of solar energy.

Q7. Why do we observe phases of moon?
Ans.

1. We observe that the everyday shape and size of the moon appears to change gradually.
2. This is because of the changes, in the relative position of the earth and the moon, with respect to sun.
3. The different appearances of moon on different days are known as the phases of the moon.

Q8. State two uses to which artificial satellite are being put?
Ans.

1. They are used in communication for transmitting radio, telephone and television signals.
2. They are also used for weather forecasting and remote sensing.

Q9. What is geo-stationary satellite?
Ans. The satellite that now makes it possible to have a live view of an event, in any part of the world, are very special satellite. They complete one orbit round in 24 hours. Scientist refers to them geo-stationary satellites.

Q10. What is solar system?
Ans. The collection of the sun, the planets, their Moons and other celestial bodies linked to the sun are known as solar system.

CHAPTER TWELVE

Observing the Sky

Fill in the blanks:-

1 A group of stars that appear to form a pattern in the sky is known as **constellation.**
2 A planet is **closer** to us rather than stars.
3 The planets are also known as **wandering stars.**
4 The pole star defines **the North** direction.
5 Stars **twinkle** but planets do not **twinkle.**
6 The planet that can seen in the evening sky, even with unaided eye is **mercury.**
7 The two stars, at the top of Ursa major, are called **pointers.**
8 The Cassiopeia is a constellation visible in **autumn**.
9 The brightest planet in the night sky is **Venus.**
10 Stars appears to move **from east to west**.
11 The planet **Saturn** was the first planet discovered by using a telescope.
12 Constellation visible in winter is **Arion**
13 Constellation visible in spring is **Ursa Major**
14 Constellation visible in autumn **Cassiopeia**
15 The morning star is **Mercury & Venus**
16 A star useful to travelers since ancient times **Pole Star.**
17 A star of average brightness **Sun.**

Question / Answers

Q1. Why do we usually not see the stars during the day?
Ans. We do not see the stars during the day because the sun dominates the day-time sky with its brightness.

Q2. In which part of the sky are we likely to find Venus when it is visible as an evening star?
Ans. Venus is seen very low near the horizon in the sky.

Q3. State the cause of the apparent motion of the sun from east to west?
Ans. Sun appears to rise in the east and to set in the west. This apparent motion of the sun for us is because of the rotation of the earth on its axis from west to east.

Q4. Name the special star in the northern hemisphere. Why has it been useful for travelers?
Ans. 1. Pole Star is a special star present in the Northern hemisphere.
2. This star unlike other appears to remain fixed at one place.
3. Because of this special features, this star has useful to travelers. It defines the North Directions.

Q5. Defines the term "Constellation"?
Ans. A constellation is a group of stars that appears to from some recognizable pattern or shape in the sky.

Q6. In what respect is the pole star different from other stars?
Ans. 1. Pole star "Dhruvtara " is a special star present in the northern hemisphere.
2. This unlike other stars appears to remains fixed at one place.
3. It ties the axis of the rotation of the earth.
4. It defines North Direction.

Q7. Write two points planets are different from other stars?

Ans.

Planet --> A planet is closer to us. Planets appears like tiny disc. Planets are not twinkling. Planets change their relative position with each other.

Star --> Stars are very far away from us. Stars appear as points. Stars are twinkling. Stars do not change their relative position with each other.

Q8. Why do stars appear to slightly shift their position in night sky?

Ans. Stars appear to slightly shift their position in the night sky due to the rotation of earth on its axis from west to east.

Q9. Why do star appears as point to us?

Ans. Stars appears as point to us because they are very far away from us.

Q10. Why Pluto is not considered a planet now?

Ans. Pluto did not considered as planet as it does not satisfy the basic characteristics of the definition of a planet.

Q11. Why do we see a new set of stars in the sky after every six months?

Ans. We see a whole different set of stars in the sky after every six months This is because the earth revolves around the sun and in six months time move to the other side of the sun.

Q12. What kind of light does the sun emit? Do all stars emit the same kind of light?

Ans. Sun shines with a yellowish white light all the other stars are however not yellowish white stars vary in size, brightness, temperature, and colour the hottest star shine with whiter blue light.

CHAPTER THIRTEEN

Practice Test

All question are of 2 marks and fillips 1 marks.

Q1. What is stepwell?
Q2. What are amphibious animals?
Q3. What is germination?
Q4. How do plants drink water?
Q6. Define the function of seed coat?
Q7. What is the function of cotyledons?
Q8. How ground water is drawn out of the tube well?
Q9. Draw picture of bean seed with label?
Q10. Write two disadvantages due to fossil fuel?
Q11. Give reason:-

- CNG is a better fuel?

Q12. Define the following:-

- Hydro- Electrocity   2. Fuels   3. Fossil Fuel.

Q13. Define term terrestrial planet?
Q14. Write two uses of artificial satellites?
Q15. State the conditions required for existence of life on a planet?
Q16. What is breathing?
Q17. Define joints? Name type of joints?

Q18. Why is bone marrow known as the factory for making blood cells?
Q19. How are fore limbs connected to the spine?
Q20. What is vegetative reproduction?
Q21. State the role of inner ear in the process of hearing?

Fill in the blanks (15)

1 _____ Ear help to maintain balance in our body.
2 The last two pair of ribs is called _____.
3 The _____ lung is slightly larger than the _____ lung.
4 The back bone protects the _____
5 _____ Is the smallest bone in our body.
6 _____ is a small hole present in the seed.

7. Movement of seeds from one place to another is called _____

8 The small baby plant coming out of a seed is known as the _____.

9 The process, by which a plant make its own food is known as _____

10 Photo means _____ and Synthesis means _____".
11 Deforestation result in _____.
12 Bee wax is used to make _____.
13 Water trapped between underground rocks is called _____.
14 _____ are aquatic plants.

MID TERM Test Paper --- 1

Fill in the blanks:-

1. Movement of seeds from one place to another is called **Seed dispersal.**
2. Lotus seeds are dispersal through **Water.**
3. **Grapes, Rose** plant which reproduce through stem cutting.
4. **Stomata** are tiny pores present on the undersurface of leaves.

Q1. Write short note on cotyledon? And draw the structure of bean seed?

Q2. Write atleast two natural ways of seed dispersal. Two example of each?
Ans. 1. Dispersal by wind :- cotton seed, Madar Seed, and Dandelion Seed.
2. Dispersal by water :- Lotus, Coconut, Water Lily.

Q3. Write two ways of reproduction?
Ans. Reproduction through underground stem :- ginger, Potato, banana.
Reproduction through Stem :- Rose, Grapes.

Q4. Why do some plants feed on Insects?
Ans. Some plants feed on insects as :-

1. These plants grow in poor soil which lacks nitrogen salt.
2. They get their extra nourishment from insects.

Q5. State the Importance of vegetative reproduction in plants?
Ans.1. It is an easier and faster method of increasing the number of the same plant.
 2 it also helps to grow plants like Banana which have no seeds.

Q6. State the necessary conditions for seed germination?
Ans. Air, Water and warmth Temperature.

Q7. Give two example of each:-

1. **Reproduction through root**:- sweet potato, Dahlia
2. **Reproduction through underground stem** :- potato, Ginger, Banana
3. **Dispersal by cracking & bursting** :- Pea, Ladyfinger
4. **Insectivorous Plants:**- Venus flytrap, Pitcher Plant

Q6. List four harmful effects of deforestation.
Ans. 1. Decrease in rainfall

2. Increase in the amount of carbon dioxide in the atmosphere that can increase global warming.
3. Decrease in the levels of ground water in the nearby areas.

    4 Increase in soil erosion that can cause more frequent floods.

Q9. Why the forests known as the "Lungs of earth"?
Ans. Forest are earth's air purifiers. They are often referred to as the earth's lungs. Just as our lungs abrob carbon dioxide from the blood and infuse it with oxygen, green plants absorb carbon dioxide during photosynthesis and in return, release oxygen into the atmosphere.

Q10. Fill Ups:-

A. The leaf, used to make disposable plates is the **areca nut leaf**.
B. Deforestation result in **Soil erosion**.
C. Bee wax is used to make **medicines**.
D. Tendu leaf is also known as **Green Gold of Odisha**.
E. A **forest** is an area where the earth is covered mainly by large number of trees.
F. **A Sanctuary** is reserved area in which birds and animal are protected from hunting.
G. The Forest Conservation Act was enacted by **the Indian Parliament in 1980**.

H. <u>Gir National Park</u> is the only place for Asiatic Lions is protected.

Q11. Match The following:-

1. Resins   à Paint
2. Forests   à Soil conservators
3. Deforestation   à Cutting down of trees
4. Aswagandha   à Medicinal plant
5. Gums   à Adhesives

Q12. Fill ups:-

1. Deforestation result in Soil erosion, low rainfall and flood.
2. Only 20% of the world's ancient forests are left.
3. A light weight narrow boat is Canoe
4. If forests disappear, the amount of carbon dioxide in air will increase.
5. Migratory Birds:- Siberian Cranes, Barons
6. National Parks :- Kaziranga, Gir
7. Birds Sanctuary :- Bharatpur, Chilka
8. Medicinal Plantts:- Amla, Ashwagandha

Q11. What is deforestation?
Ans:- Large scale cutting of trees is called deforestation.

Q12. State the importance of forest to human beings?
Ans. 1. Trees purify the air by absorbing carbon dioxide and releasing
   oxygen.
    2 Forest help to bring good rainfall.
    3 Forest prevent soil erosion.

4 Trees also help in checking the global warming by absorbing carbon dioxide which is main greenhouse gas.

www.ingramcontent.com/pod-product-compliance
Lightning Source LLC
LaVergne TN
LVHW021737060526
838200LV00052B/3327